THE KIDS' BOOK OF
Questions
&
Answers

FASCINATING FACTS ABOUT NATURE, SCIENCE, SPACE AND MUCH MORE!

by Ian Graham & Dr. Paul Sterry

COURAGE BOOKS

AN IMPRINT OF RUNNING PRESS
PHILADELPHIA • LONDON

The Kids' Book of Questions and Answers
Fascinating Facts about Nature, Science, Space, and Much More!

Copyright © 1996 by Andromeda Oxford Limited

First published in the United States in 1998 by Courage Books

Printed in Hong Kong.

9 8 7 6 5 4 3 2 1
Digit on the right indicates the number of this printing

Library of Congress Cataloging-in-Publication Number
97-66810

ISBN 0-7624-0280-6

Planned and produced by
Andromeda Oxford Limited
11–15 The Vineyard
Abingdon
Oxon OX14 3PX
England

Published by Courage Books, an imprint of
Running Press Book Publishers
125 South Twenty-second Street
Philadelphia, Pennsylvania 19103-4399

CONTENTS

STARS & GALAXIES

Q What is a constellation?

A A constellation is a group of stars. Ancient astronomers gave many of them names, because they thought their patterns in the night sky made shapes that reminded them of things such as animals and gods. Many constellations are visible on a clear night. Some of these are shown below. There are 88 constellations.

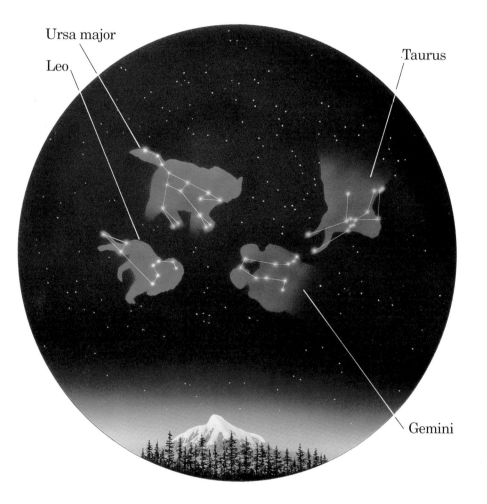

Ursa major

Leo

Taurus

Gemini

Q What is a solar eclipse?

A As the Earth orbits the Sun, and the Moon orbits the Earth, all three sometimes line up. A solar eclipse (above) occurs when the Moon passes in front of the Sun and blocks out its light.

Q What shape is the Milky Way?

A The Sun is one of 100 billion stars that form a galaxy called the Milky Way. If we could look at the Milky Way from the outside, it would look like a glowing ball surrounded by a thin disk of curling arms. We live in one of the galaxy's arms. Because of its shape, the Milky Way is called a spiral galaxy.

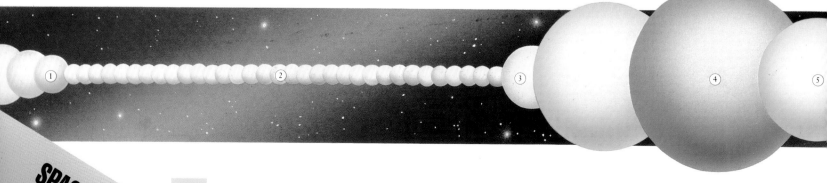

Q How was our Solar System formed?

A About 4.6 billion years ago, a cloud of gas and dust began to spiral inward on itself (1). The center of the cloud heated up (2) and matter streamed out from its poles (3). The spinning cloud flattened into a disk (4). The hot core became the Sun. The planets formed from clumps of matter in the disk (5).

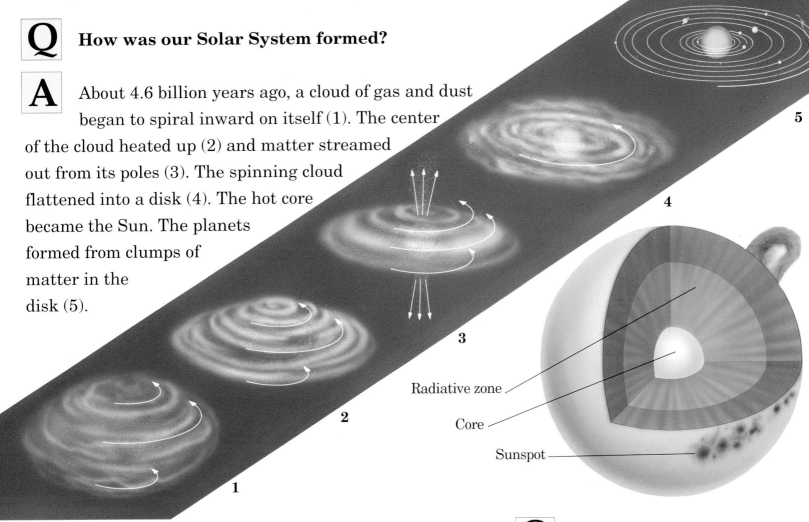

5

4

3

2

1

Radiative zone

Core

Sunspot

Q Where did the galaxies come from?

A The universe began about 15 billion years ago in an explosion called The "Big Bang." Matter formed in the explosion collected together in clouds. The clouds collapsed inwards and formed clumps of stars, the galaxies, spinning through space.

Q What is a star?

A A star, like the Sun (above), is a large, burning ball of gases. The gas is mostly hydrogen. The hydrogen atoms are packed so tightly in the star's core that they join together to make a different gas, helium. This process, called nuclear fusion, releases an enormous amount of energy, which produces heat and light.

6

7

Q How does a star die?

A When a star like the Sun (left) burns all of its hydrogen, it begins to die. It puffs up to form a star called a red giant. It then shrinks and cools to become a tiny white dwarf star.

THE PLANETS

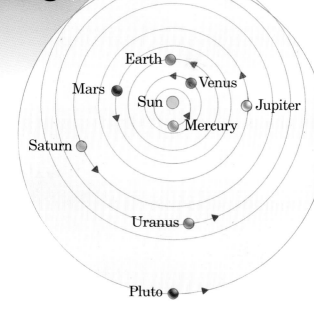

Q What are planets made of?

A The planets that are closest to the Sun, from Mercury to Mars, are small, rocky worlds. They have a metal center, or core, surrounded by a thick mantle of rock with a thin, rocky crust on the surface. The outer planets are very different. Jupiter and Saturn are made mostly of hydrogen. Uranus and Neptune have a rocky core surrounded by ice and hydrogen (below). Pluto is made of rock, with an icy coating.

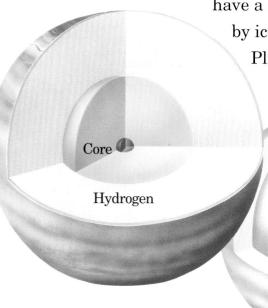

Core

Hydrogen

Saturn

Core

Hydrogen and ice

Uranus

Q How do the planets orbit the Sun?

A All the planets in the Solar System travel in the same direction around the Sun (above). Their paths are slightly flattened circles called ellipses. Pluto's orbit is pushed so much to one side that it crosses Neptune's orbit

Q What are planets?

A Planets are worlds that orbit the Sun. The word "planet" comes from a Greek word meaning wanderer, because of the strange wandering paths they appear to have when seen from Earth. There are nine planets (right). Mercury is the closest to the Sun, then Venus, Earth, Mars, Jupiter, Saturn, Uranus, Neptune and Pluto.

Mercury   Venus   Earth   Mars   Jupiter

Q What is the Great Red Spot?

A Jupiter's Great Red Spot (below) is a swirling storm 18,600 miles across. It was first seen by astronomers as long ago as 1664. Storms on Earth last a few weeks at most. The Great Red Spot has lasted for centuries because Jupiter has no solid surface to slow it down.

Great Red Spot

Q Which planets have moons?

A Only Mercury and Venus do not have moons. Earth has one moon. Mars has two (above). Jupiter has 16 moons. One of them, Ganymede, is larger than the planet Mercury. Saturn has 19 moons, Uranus 15, Neptune eight while Pluto has only one.

Q Is there life on other planets?

A Most of the planets are too harsh to support life as we know it. For many years, people thought that there might be life on Mars. Some astronomers thought they saw lines and dark patches on the planet that might be canals carrying water to grow plants. But when two Viking spacecraft landed there in 1976 and tested the soil, they found no signs of life.

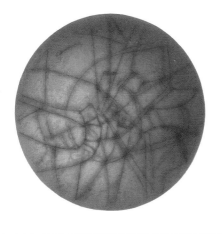

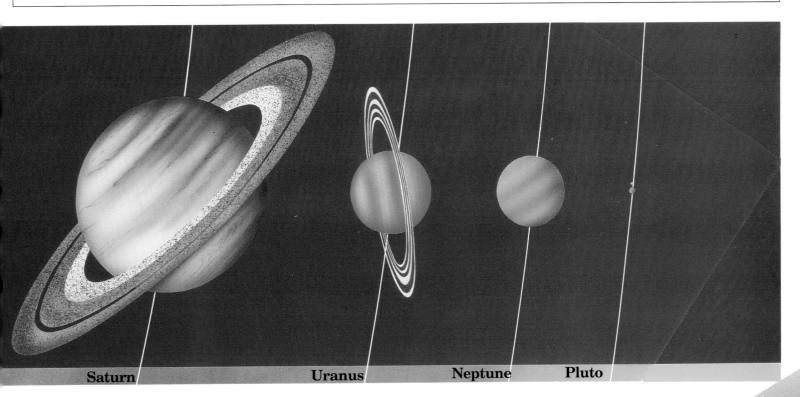

Saturn   Uranus   Neptune   Pluto

SPACE

EXPLORING THE HEAVENS

Q **How did early astronomers study the heavens?**

A Astronomers studied the sky with the naked eye until the 17th century. In 1609 the Italian astronomer Galileo Galilei (above) became the first person to study the sky with a telescope.

Q **What did Giotto tell us about comets?**

A In 1986, the Giotto space probe (below) studied Halley's Comet. A comet consists of a lump of rock and ice called the nucleus, inside a cloud of gas and dust called the coma (inset). It also has a bright tail. Giotto's photographs show a nucleus measuring 5 miles by 7.4 miles. Its instruments found that the coma and tail are made of dust and water vapor.

Q **How does a modern telescope work?**

A There are two types of telescope. A refractor uses a lens to form an image. A reflector uses a curved mirror. Most modern telescopes used in astronomy are reflectors. The telescope is finely balanced and turns slowly to keep the image steady as the Earth moves. A Schmidt telescope (right) is used to photograph large areas of the sky.

Schmidt telescope gathering light from the stars

Counterbalance

Inside the telescope

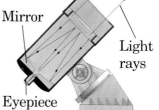

Mirror

Light rays

Eyepiece

Q Why is the Hubble telescope in space?

A Light from distant stars passes through the Earth's atmosphere before it reaches a telescope on the ground. The swirling atmosphere makes the stars twinkle. Modern telescopes are usually built on top of mountains, where the atmosphere is thinner, to reduce this effect. The Hubble Space Telescope (below) can see more clearly than any telescope on Earth because it is above the atmosphere.

Q Where did the Voyager space probes go?

A Voyager 1 and 2 were launched in 1977. The pull of gravity from the outer planets guided the spacecraft from one planet to the next. Voyager 1 flew past Jupiter in 1979 (below) and Saturn in 1980. Voyager 2 flew past Jupiter (1979), Saturn (1981), Uranus (1986) and Neptune (1989). Their cameras and instruments studied each planet. All the information was sent back to Earth by radio.

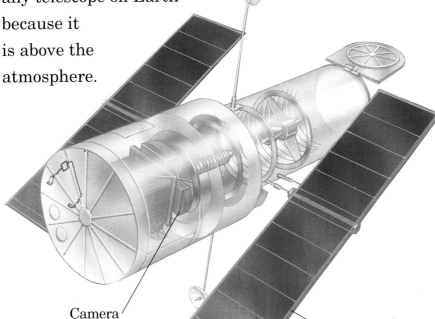

Camera

Solar panel

Q How did the Pioneer space probes work?

A Pioneer 10 and 11 were the first spacecraft to visit the outer Solar System. They were designed to find out if a spacecraft could travel through the asteroid belt, a swarm of rocks orbiting the Sun between Mars and Jupiter. Most spacecraft use solar cells to make electricity from sunlight. Pioneer 10 and 11 traveled so far from the Sun that solar cells would not work. Instead, they carried nuclear power generators to make electricity.

Pioneer 11

Thruster

Cosmic ray telescope

Nuclear power generator

SPACE

MAN IN SPACE

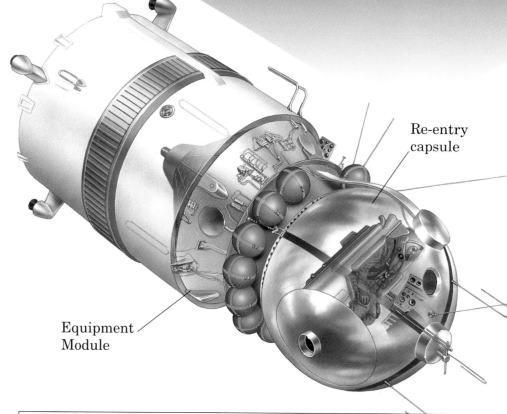

Re-entry capsule

Equipment Module

Q Who was the first man in space?

A The first man in space was Yuri Gagarin from the former Soviet Union. On April 12, 1961, his tiny Vostok space capsule (left), only 7½ feet across, made one orbit of the Earth. The spherical capsule then separated from its Equipment Module and rocket before plunging back into the Earth's atmosphere and landing by parachute.

Q How did astronauts land on the Moon?

A Apollo astronauts traveled to the Moon in a spacecraft made from three modules linked together. They lived in the cone-shaped Command Module. A Service Module supplied it with oxygen and electric power. Once they were in orbit around the Moon, two of the three astronauts moved into the Lunar Module. They separated it from the rest of the spacecraft and landed on the Moon.

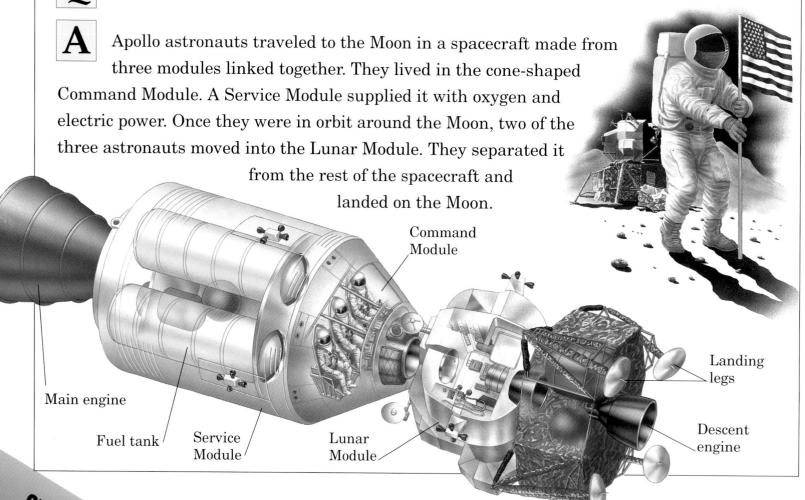

Command Module

Main engine

Fuel tank

Service Module

Lunar Module

Landing legs

Descent engine

Q How do cosmonauts return to Earth?

A Before the Space Shuttle, all American manned spacecraft landed in the Pacific Ocean. Russian Soyuz spacecraft (below) are brought down on land. The small Re-entry Module descends through the atmosphere by parachute. Just before it touches the ground, rockets in the base of the spacecraft fire to cushion the landing.

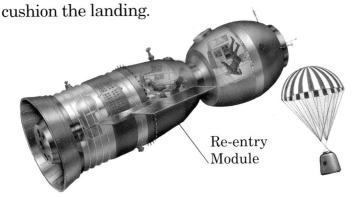

Re-entry Module

Q How does the Space Shuttle take off?

A Six seconds before lift-off, three rocket engines in the Space Shuttle's tail fire. They burn fuel supplied by the huge fuel tank underneath the spacecraft (below). Then the rocket boosters on each side of the fuel tank fire. Clamps holding the spacecraft down on the launch-pad are released and the Space Shuttle takes off.

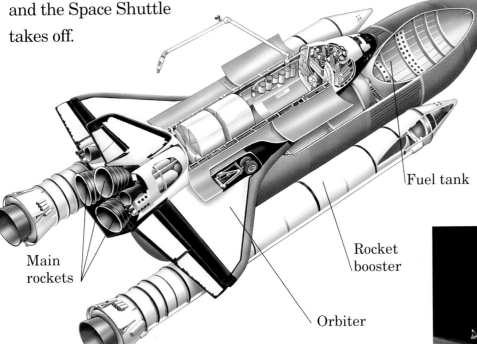

Main rockets

Fuel tank

Rocket booster

Orbiter

Q How is a space station built?

A A space station is far too big to launch in one piece. Instead, it is launched in sections that have to be connected together in space. The Russian space station Mir (right) was launched in four pieces. The base unit was launched first in 1986. It was followed by three more modules that were linked to the base unit.

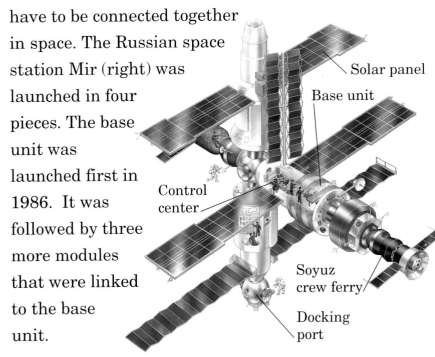

Solar panel

Base unit

Control center

Soyuz crew ferry

Docking port

Q What will spacecraft look like in the future?

A Future spacecraft will probably be powered by new types of engines instead of rockets. The ramscoop (below) collects hydrogen atoms from space in a large funnel and its engine fuses them together to release energy. The photon sail (bottom) is "blown" through space by light from the Sun or lasers.

SPACE

THE EARTH

Q What is beneath the Earth's surface?

A The Earth's inner core (below) is a solid ball about 1,500 miles across made of iron and nickel. This is surrounded by an outer core about 1,400 miles thick made of molten iron and nickel. Outside this lies the mantle, made from rock about 1,900 miles thick. The outside layer is a thin rocky crust up to 50 miles thick.

Q What are volcanoes?

A Volcanoes are holes in the Earth's crust which allow molten rock to escape from beneath. The molten rock, or lava, may flow out gently or it may be blasted high in the air with gas and ash in a violent explosion. When volcanic eruptions pile up the lava into a cone-shaped mountain (below), this is also called a volcano.

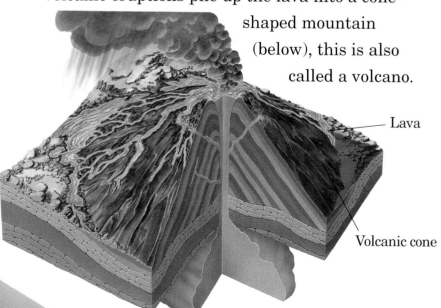

— Lava

Volcanic cone

Q Is the seabed flat?

A Underneath the world's oceans (above), the seabed is divided by mountain ridges up to 2.5 miles high, 2,500 miles wide and 25,000 miles long. Molten rock constantly erupts at the ridges, forming a new seabed which spreads out on each side.

Q What is a rift valley?

A When magma, or lava, wells up underground, it pushes up the crust above it, stretching and cracking the surface. The cracked crust sinks and forms a valley with steep sides and a flat bottom, called a rift valley. The valley may flood with water to form a new ocean.

Q Why do rivers flow?

A Rivers flow because water runs downhill. Mountain streams fed by rain or melting snow meet and form a river (below). Streams that flow into rivers are called tributaries. Further down, where the slope is gentler, the river is slower and wider. Finally, it flows out into the sea.

Q What is continental drift?

A Continental drift is the movement of Earth's land masses. There was once a single continent which we call Pangaea. The rest of the Earth was covered with water. About 200 million years ago, Pangaea split up. The pieces slowly drifted apart and became today's continents (above).

Q Where are the world's highest mountains?

A Mountains are formed by movements of the Earth's crust. The edges of continents are pushed and squeezed together, thrusting up the land in the process. The highest mountain range is the Himalayas (below). Its highest peak is Mount Everest (29,028 feet above sea level).

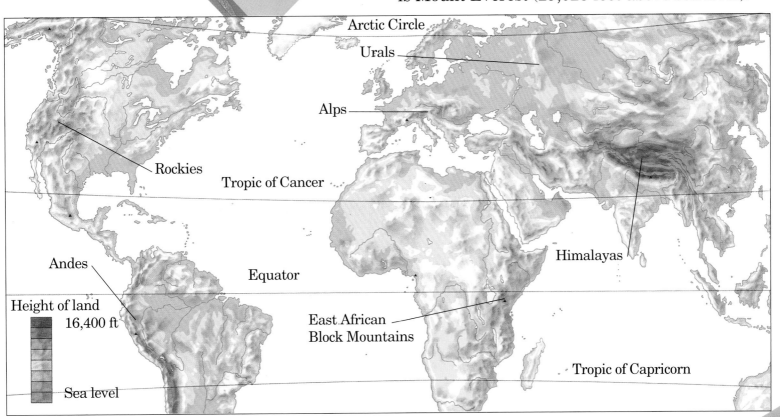

Arctic Circle

Urals

Alps

Rockies

Tropic of Cancer

Andes

Equator

East African
Block Mountains

Himalayas

Height of land
16,400 ft

Sea level

Tropic of Capricorn

OUR WORLD

ROCKS & MINERALS

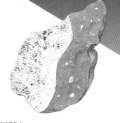

Tillite

Marble

Syenite

 Q **What are the main types of rocks?**

 A There are three main types of rock—igneous, sedimentary and metamorphic (above). Igneous rock such as syenite is solidified lava. Sedimentary rock such as tillite is formed from compressed particles. Metamorphic rock such as marble is made from rock changed by heat or pressure.

Q **How do we obtain rocks and minerals?**

A Rocks and minerals are taken out of the ground by mining (below). If they are near the surface, they can be mined by scraping the earth away. This is open cast or strip mining. Deeper minerals are mined by shaft mining. Deep shafts are dug and miners tunnel out from the shafts to extract the minerals.

Q **What is a mineral?**

A Rocks are made from minerals. Each mineral is made from a different set of chemicals. Most rocks contain several minerals. Olivine is a green mineral found in basalt. Quartz is the most common mineral on Earth. Galena contains lead.

Olivine

Galena

Quartz

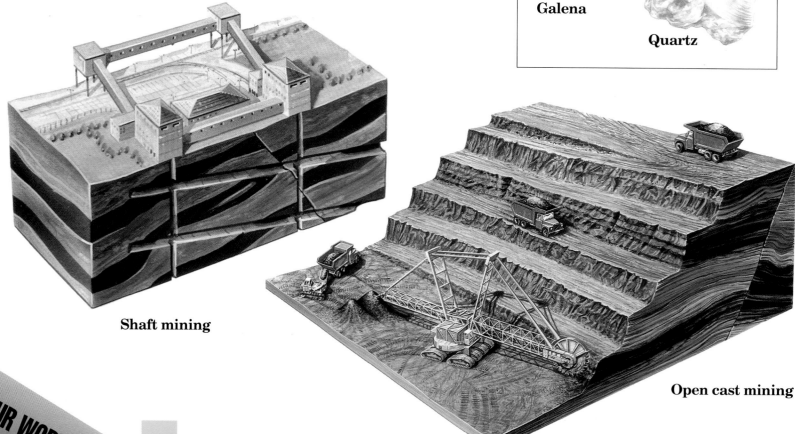

Shaft mining

Open cast mining

Q How did ancient people use stone?

A People have used stone for making things since prehistoric times. The first humans made axes and knives from flint. The Egyptians built stone pyramids to house the bodies of their kings. The Ancient Greeks built temples to their gods. The roofs were supported by massive stone columns. The Romans carved stone statues of their gods and leaders (right).

Pyramid building

Greek column

Roman statue

Q What are fossils?

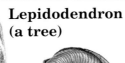

Lepidodendron (a tree)

A Fossils are the remains of prehistoric animals and plants preserved in rock. When an animal or plant died, it sometimes sank into soil or mud. The animal or plant rotted away and its shape was replaced by minerals.

Ammonite (a shell)

Sea-lily

Q How are rocks changed by heat?

A When hot, molten magma forces its way up through the Earth's crust (below), it changes the surrounding rocks. For example, limestone, which is soft and crumbly, becomes harder and changes into marble. The rising magma is called an igneous intrusion.

Q What are gems?

A Gems are rare and beautiful stones found in the Earth's crust. Most are crystals made of minerals. Opal and amethyst are two forms of silica. Sapphire is made of corundum. Diamond is made from a single element—carbon. Gems are cut to size, polished and made into jewelry with gold or silver (below).

Diamond

Diamond ring

Opal

Sapphire

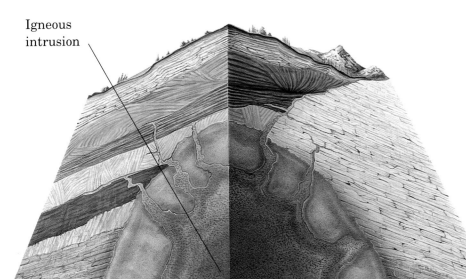

Amethyst

Igneous intrusion

OUR WORLD

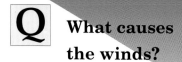 ENVIRONMENT

Q What causes the winds?

A Winds are created because of differences in air temperature and air pressure. When air is heated at the Equator (below), it rises, cools and then sinks over the tropics. Some moves back again towards the equator, creating the trade winds. The rest is drawn towards the poles as westerly winds.

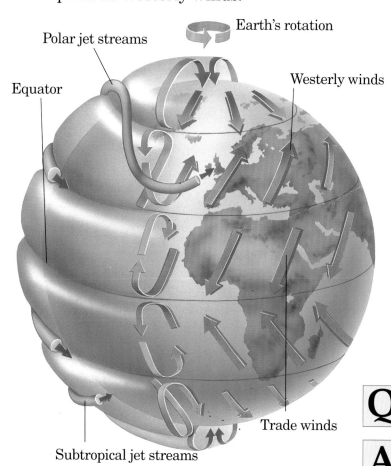

Earth's rotation

Polar jet streams

Westerly winds

Equator

Trade winds

Subtropical jet streams

Water vapor in clouds

Water falls as rain

Q How are clouds formed?

A Water evaporates from land, lakes and sea (above) and is carried by the air as water vapor. Warm air can hold more water vapor than cold air. As warm air rises and cools, for example over a mountain, the water vapor condenses to water, forming clouds. Eventually, the water falls from the clouds as rain. The rainwater runs back into the rivers and lakes.

Q What is erosion?

A Erosion is the breaking down of solid rock into smaller particles which are then carried away. Wind, water, gravity, sea and rain are common natural causes of erosion and so is ice (below). The frozen ice in the glacier carves U-shaped valleys as it moves slowly downhill. Most mountain valleys are formed in this way. Today, human activity also causes damaging erosion.

Ice

Water

Gravity

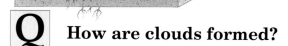

Wind

Sea

Q What is energy conservation?

A We use a lot of energy in our homes. Much of it comes from oil, coal or gas, which are fossil fuels that will one day be used up. If we insulate our houses better, and trap the Sun's heat, we use less fuel. This is called energy conservation. We can also use ever-lasting energy sources, such as wind (below).

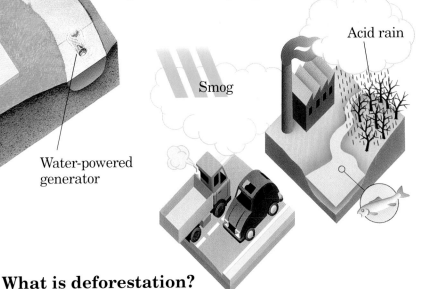

Solar panel

Heat insulation

Wind-powered generator

Water-powered generator

Methane generator

Q Why is pollution harmful?

A Many of the fumes and chemicals produced by cars or industry (below) can damage plants and animals. Even small amounts of some polluting gases or liquids can kill large numbers of living things and many are also poisonous to people as well.

Acid rain

Smog

Q What is deforestation?

A Forests once covered about 15 billion acres of the Earth but now only 10 billion acres are left (below). The process of cutting down trees is called deforestation, and is carried out by people. Trees are important to our survival because, like other green plants, they produce oxygen. Without oxygen, animals cannot survive.

Q How does the peppered moth adapt to pollution?

A The peppered moth rests on tree bark where its camouflage hides it from bird predators. The bark in polluted towns may be black and normal camouflage would be useless. In these areas, a black-winged form of the moth is found.

Normal form   **Black-winged form**

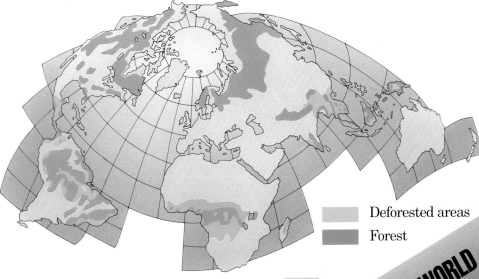

Deforested areas

Forest

EVOLUTION

Q What is evolution?

A The first forms of life appeared on Earth many hundreds of millions of years ago. They were tiny, primitive creatures that lived in water. As millions of years went by, these creatures gradually changed and many different forms of life slowly appeared (above). This process is called evolution and it is still continuing today.

Q What does extinction mean?

A Extinction occurs when the last individual of a plant or animal species dies out. In the past, many creatures such as dinosaurs died out naturally—perhaps because of changes in the climate. In the last few centuries, animals such as the dodo (left) and the thylacine (below) have been hunted to extinction by people.

Q How do we know about the past?

A We find out about the past from fossils. If a prehistoric animal died in shallow, muddy water, its body might become covered with layers of silt which eventually formed solid rock. The soft parts decayed but the skeleton slowly absorbed minerals and hardened in the rock to become a fossil (left). Millions of years later, if the rock is worn away, we can find the fossils.

Q What is natural selection?

A Not all animals are as strong as others of the same species. This deer was not fast enough to escape a tiger attack and it will be killed. Other, fitter deer will evade capture and survive to breed. This process of survival of the fittest is called natural selection.

Q How did the horse evolve?

A The horse evolved from a rabbit-sized animal called *Hyracotherium* that lived 50 million years ago. Its descendants such as *Mesohippus* and *Merychippus* grew larger and became grazing animals. The number of toes in the foot dwindled from four to one, which improved its running speed, and eventually the modern horse (below) evolved.

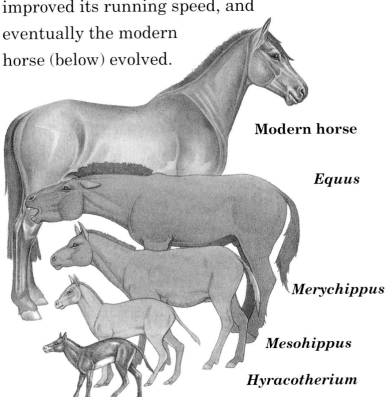

Modern horse

Equus

Merychippus

Mesohippus

Hyracotherium

Q What is adaptation?

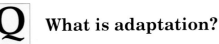

A Animals and plants often develop traits that help them survive. Such traits are called adaptations. This tree-living tarsier is adapted with long legs for leaping, sucker-like clinging toes and large eyes for seeing at night.

Q When did our ancestors evolve?

A Our first true ancestor was the ape-like *Ramapithecus* (right). It lived about 8 million years ago, mainly in trees, but also foraged on the ground for food. Fossil bones have been found in Africa, Europe and India. *Australopithecus*, the next link in the chain, lived some 3 million years ago in East Africa.

PREHISTORIC LIFE

Q What were the first animals like?

A The first animals were probably single-celled creatures. Their bodies had no hard parts so they did not form fossils. The first animals that we know from fossils lived 570 million years ago. Many had worm-like or plant-like bodies. Others had armored head shields (below).

Q How did *Pterodactylus* fly?

A *Pterodactylus* (above) had a lightweight, furry body and was able to fly using its long, membranous wings. These were attached to the wrist bones and the bones of the fourth finger. *Pterodactylus* probably clung to cliff edges and then launched itself into the air, where it glided over the sea snatching fish from the surface.

Q What did prehistoric fish eat?

A Although no one can be completely sure, the diet of prehistoric fish probably consisted of worm-like creatures and mollusks. Some of the larger species of fish had numerous sharp teeth. They might have chased and eaten other fish, in a similar way to modern-day sharks and barracuda.

Cryptoclidus

Ichthyosaurus

Peloneustes

Q Which reptiles ruled the seas?

A In ancient times, the seas were ruled by ichthyosaurs and plesiosaurs (above). Both had streamlined bodies and paddle-shaped limbs. *Ichthyosaurus* resembled a cross between a fish and a dolphin. Some plesiosaurs, such as *Cryptoclidus,* had long necks; others, like *Peloneustes*, were whale-like. Ichthyosaurs and plesiosaurs ate mainly fish, but some plesiosaurs also ate one another.

Q How did mammals survive the Ice Age?

A As the Ice Age approached and the climate became colder, many mammals grew larger. This is because large animals retain their body heat better than small ones. Heat retention was also helped by growing thick, furry coats, such as that seen in the woolly mammoth (left). Thick layers of fat beneath the skin provided insulation. Other large, hairy mammals that survived the Ice Age included woolly rhinoceroses and giant cave bears.

Q What were the terror cranes?

A Terror cranes were giant birds that lived some 50 million years ago in North America. They stood 6½ feet tall and hunted small mammals in areas of open grassland. They had strong legs for running and a powerful, hook-tipped bill for dealing with their prey. Terror cranes are given the scientific name *Diatryma.*

NATURE

DINOSAURS

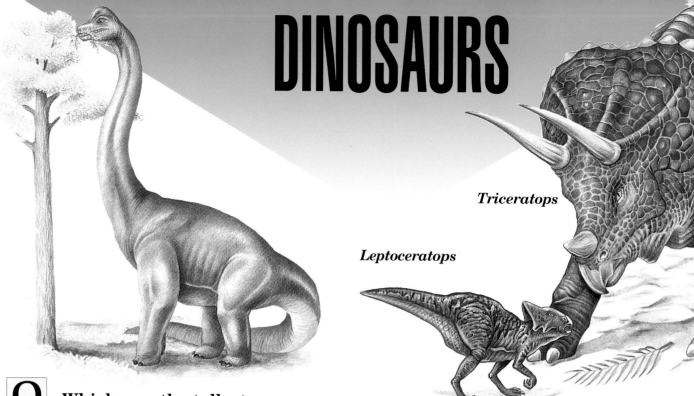

Triceratops

Leptoceratops

Q Which was the tallest dinosaur?

A Many of the huge, plant-eating dinosaurs had long necks. The tallest was *Brachiosaurus* (above) which not only had a long neck but long front legs as well. It could stretch up to 40 feet and probably fed on the tops of trees, much as giraffes do today. It needed legs the size of tree trunks to support its great weight.

Q Why did some dinosaurs have armoured heads?

A Some dinosaurs were meat-eating predators. Not surprisingly, many of the plant-eating dinosaurs developed armored heads to help defend themselves (above). The head of *Triceratops* was covered with a large plate and carried three, forward-pointing horns. *Leptoceratops* was much smaller and lacked *Triceratops'* horns.

Q Which was the most fearsome meat-eater?

A *Tyrannosaurus* (right) was probably the most terrifying carnivorous dinosaur. It was certainly one of the largest. The head was huge and its skull was larger than a man. *Tyrannosaurus* stood upright on massive hind legs and could outrun slower, plant-eating dinosaurs. Its teeth, which were 6 inches long, were used to rip and tear the flesh of its prey.

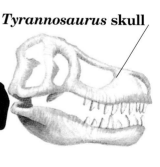

Tyrannosaurus **skull**

Q How did *Stegosaurus* get warm?

A *Stegosaurus* was a large, 25-foot-long dinosaur with a double row of armored plates on its back. These may have been useful in defense but were probably also used to control body temperature. They would have gathered heat from the Sun's rays to warm *Stegosaurus* up. Breezes passing through the plates would have helped *Stegosaurus* cool off if it was too hot.

Q Were all dinosaurs big?

A Although some dinosaurs were the largest land animals ever to have lived, many were tiny. Among the smallest were species of *Compsognathus* (left). Some were the size of a chicken. Most *Compsognathus* species had long legs and were good runners. This one is trying to catch a dragonfly.

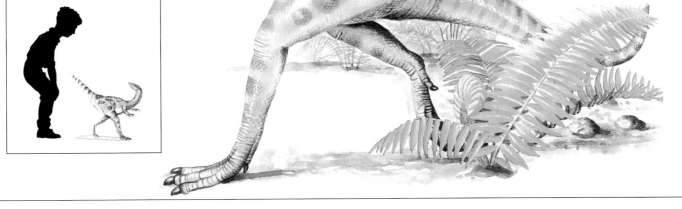

Q How do we know what dinosaurs looked like?

A We can tell what dinosaurs looked like from fossils. These are found in sedimentary rocks from all over the world. Often just a few dinosaur bones are found but sometimes scientists discover a complete skeleton.

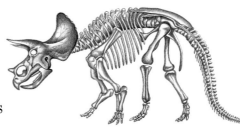

NATURE

INSECTS & SPIDERS

Q **How does the praying mantis get its name?**

A The praying mantis (below) is a fierce, predatory insect that catches other insects for food. Its front pair of legs are specially adapted for grabbing prey. As the mantis is stalking its victim, these legs are held folded under its head. When it does this, it looks as though it might be praying, and this is how it got its name.

Q **Which is the most poisonous spider?**

A Although quite small, the black widow (above) is perhaps the most deadly spider. There are several different species which live in warm areas such as North America and Australia. Because it likes dark, shady places, the spider often goes into houses. It is therefore more likely to bite people than other poisonous spiders.

Q **How do ants live?**

A Ants are insects that live in colonies. Their large underground nests (right) contain thousands of individual ants, and have a series of chambers and tunnels. One important chamber will be home to the queen ant. She lays thousands of eggs which soon hatch into ant larvae. These are first fed by the adult ants. Then they turn into pupae from which adult ants finally emerge.

Queen ant

Eggs

Worker ants keep greenfly for food

Worker ant

Larvae

Adult ants break out of pupae

Worker ant bringing food

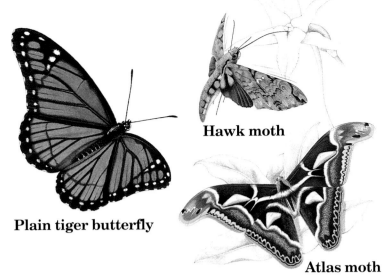

Plain tiger butterfly

Hawk moth

Atlas moth

Q How can you tell butterflies and moths apart?

A Although similar insects to look at, butterflies fly by day while moths mostly fly at night. Most butterflies have club-tipped antennae while moths usually have straight or feathery antennae (above). Butterflies usually close their wings together at rest.

Q How many different kinds of insects are there?

A Nobody knows for sure how many different insects there are. It has been estimated, however, that there may be more than 30 million types, or species, in a huge variety of shapes and sizes. Examples from the major groups, or orders, of insects are shown below.

Q Do insects have territories?

A A few insects do have territories which they defend against others of their kind. These two male stalk-eyed flies (right) from Africa are assessing each other's size by measuring their eye stalks. The prize for the winner is to mate with any female that enters the territory.

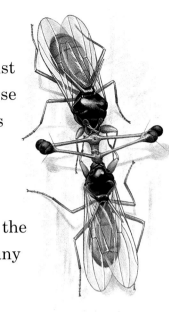

Q Why are some insects brightly colored?

A Some insects have bright colors to attract one another to mate. Others, such as this ladybird, advertise the fact that they taste nasty by being colorful. Birds and other predators soon learn to associate the color red in particular with creatures which taste nasty or which may be poisonous.

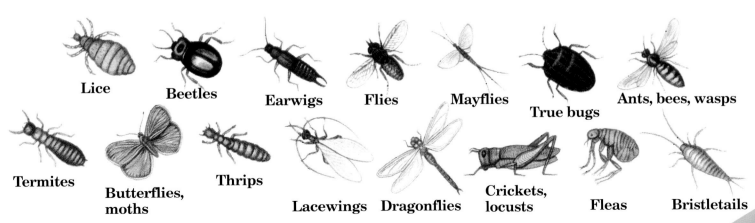

Lice **Beetles** **Earwigs** **Flies** **Mayflies** **True bugs** **Ants, bees, wasps**

Termites **Butterflies, moths** **Thrips** **Lacewings** **Dragonflies** **Crickets, locusts** **Fleas** **Bristletails**

NATURE

FISH

Q Which fish climbs trees?

A The mudskipper (below) lives in African mangrove swamps. Because it can take in oxygen through its mouth and throat, it can venture on to the mudflats when the tide is out. If danger threatens and it cannot get back to its burrow, it can climb mangrove roots to escape.

Q What is unusual about the seahorse?

A Apart from its curious shape, the seahorse (right) is unusual because it is the male and not the female which looks after the eggs and young. He has a brood pouch on his belly and this can hold up to 200 eggs and young. When the young are old enough, the male expels them from the pouch.

Q How does a fish sense its surroundings?

A Although most fish have good eyesight and a sense of taste, they also use a structure called the lateral line (right). This groove lies along the side of a fish's body, and contains special cells that are sensitive to vibrations in the water. With this, the fish can detect both food and danger.

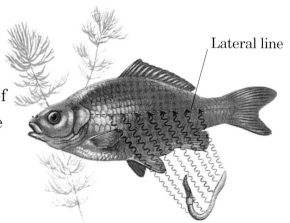

Lateral line

Q How does a shark hunt its prey?

A Although sharks have poor eyesight, they have an excellent sense of smell. They can detect blood diluted a million times in water and will home in on a wounded animal in the sea. Sharks are also able to detect vibrations in the water caused, for example, by the thrashing movements of an injured fish.

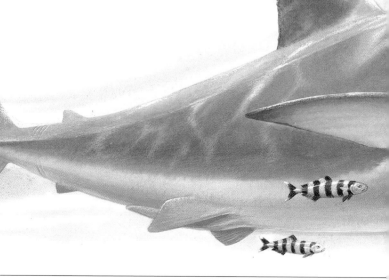

Q Which fish can spear boats?

A Although they do not do it often, swordfish (right) have been known to spear the hulls of wooden boats. They have a snout which is long and pointed. It carries rows of small, sharp teeth along the sides, like the blade of a saw. The swordfish probably uses this to slash at prey and predators.

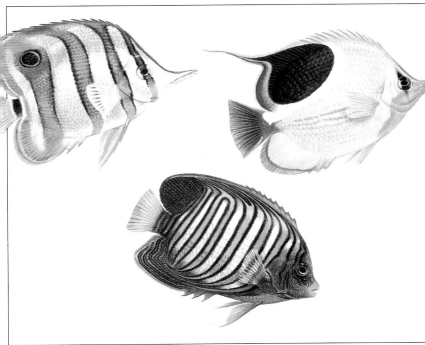

Q How do butterfly fish get their name?

A Butterfly fish get their name because they are very brightly colored, like the wings of a butterfly. Most species are found on coral reefs in tropical waters around the world. The colors and patterns are thought to confuse predators. They may also help the fish blend into its surroundings to hide from predators.

Q How does a flounder avoid its enemies?

A The flounder (below) is a flatfish that lives on the sandy seabed. Its markings and colors help it blend in with its surroundings, for camouflage. The flounder can also flick sand over its body using its fins. Often only the head and eyes remain visible.

NATURE

AMPHIBIANS & REPTILES

Q Are all snakes poisonous?

A Many snakes are perfectly harmless to humans and do not have poison fangs or venom. Although it may look menacing, this Arafura wart snake (above), which lives in rivers in Australia and New Guinea, does not have a poisonous bite.

Q What is a salamander?

A Salamanders such as this tiger salamander (right) are related to newts, and both are amphibians. Salamanders are perfectly at home on land but have to live in damp places. This is because their skins easily lose water. Some species can breed on land but many return to water to spawn. Salamanders eat small creatures such as worms and slugs.

Q How do frogs breathe?

A Like other amphibians, frogs have lungs which they use to take in air and absorb oxygen into their blood. They are also able to take up oxygen through their skins. In order to do this, however, they have to keep their bodies moist at all times. Frogs are also able to absorb oxygen through the moist lining of their mouths.

Q Which turtle travels farthest?

A Most turtles travel long distances during their lives. The green turtle (left), however, probably holds the record. Individuals that feed off the coast of South America travel 1,360 miles to Ascension Island to breed. Turtles make these long-distance journeys because the number of beaches suitable for egg-laying is small.

Q How does the collared lizard escape?

A The collared lizard (right) lives on grassy plains in North America. In order to escape from danger, the lizard is able to run on its back legs. It is able, therefore, to move at faster speeds than if it were having to scurry on all four legs.

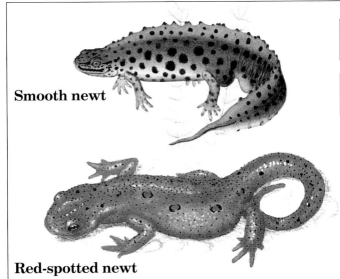

Smooth newt

Red-spotted newt

Q How do newts find their way home?

A Newts such as the smooth newt and the red-spotted newt spend much of their lives on land but return to water to breed. They often find the pond where they themselves were spawned. Most species use taste and smell to help them navigate. A few species also use the Sun or the Earth's magnetism to check the direction they are traveling in.

Q Which reptiles can change color?

A Chameleons (left) are able to change their color to match their background. They do this by moving pigment around in their skins, and the change can be complete in just a few minutes. Chameleons use this ability to change color for camouflage. This way they can avoid being spotted by predators. They can also get closer to prey without being seen.

SEA MAMMALS

Bottle-nosed dolphin

Common porpoise

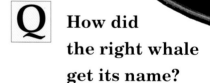

Q **What is the difference between a dolphin and a porpoise?**

A A dolphin is larger than a porpoise (above) and has a beak-nose; it also has a large hump on its forehead. The porpoise is the smallest of the whales and does not have the dolphin's "beak." Instead it has a rather stubby, rounded head. Dolphins and porpoises are both types of small whale. They feed on fish and can swim very fast to catch their prey.

Q **Which animal is called the sea canary?**

A The beluga whale (above), which lives in arctic seas, is called the sea canary. This is because it makes a wide variety of clicking and chirping noises and sometimes snaps its jaws together as well. In the summer, belugas move into the mouths of rivers to feed on migrating salmon. They sometimes gather in large numbers to feed, and their canary-like sounds can be heard from above the water as well as from below. Adult belugas are white but their young are darker in color.

Q **How did the right whale get its name?**

A Sad though it may seem, early whalers gave the right whale its name. They considered it to be the "right" whale to catch because it was a slow swimmer and floated after it had been killed. Some species of whale sink after they have been killed and would have been difficult for early whalers to tow back to their ship. Right whales were nearly hunted to extinction.

A The killer whale (below) is the most ferocious sea mammal. It eats fish, squid, sharks and even seals, porpoises and walruses. Sometimes killer whales launch themselves from the sea to snatch seals from the beach. Packs of killer whales have even been known to attack animals as large as blue whales. Surprisingly, attacks on humans have never been known, and killer whales can be watched closely from boats.

Q How does the sea otter eat clams?

A The sea otter lives in the north Pacific waters off California. It has developed a clever method of opening clams and mussel shells to reach the food inside. Lying on its back on the surface of the sea, the sea otter places a large stone on its chest. It then strikes the clam or mussel shell against the stone until the shell shatters. The sea otter can then easily reach the food inside the shell.

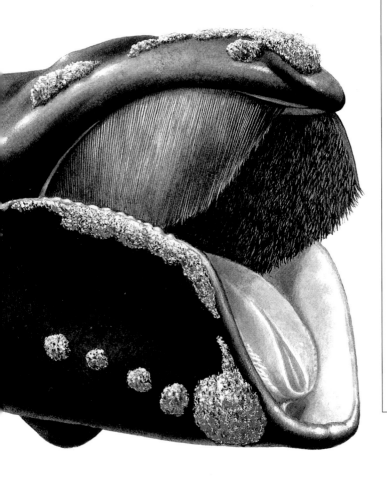

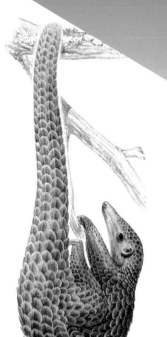

Q Which animal is called the "walking pine cone"?

A This name is used to describe the pangolin (left). It is also sometimes called the scaly anteater. Most of the pangolin's body is covered in hard, protective, overlapping scales. When threatened, it curls into a ball. Some pangolins can climb trees.

Q Which animal is called the river horse?

A The hippopotamus (above) is sometimes called the river horse. In fact its name is made up of Greek and Latin words meaning "river" and "horse." Hippos live in Africa and spend much of the day partly under the water in rivers and lakes. After dark, they may come out to feed on the plants on the bank. Hippos can be quarrelsome animals and two males will often fight one another, sometimes causing injuries.

Q What is a rhino's horn made from?

A Although it may look solid and bony, the horn of a rhino (below) has a hollow center and is made from the same material as hair and hooves. Rhinos are sometimes illegally killed for their horns, in the belief that the horn makes a good medicine. As a result, rhinos are rare and endangered today even though the trade in their horns is banned in most countries.

Q How does a mongoose defeat a cobra?

A The deadly cobra is usually no match for a mongoose. The mongoose is extremely agile, and leaps away when the snake tries to strike. Soon the snake tires, and then the mongoose attacks, killing the snake with a bite to the neck.

Q How does a lion catch its prey?

A Although its prey may be fast-moving, a lion is stealthy and will creep close to its victim before making its attack. Lions often work as a team with different individuals cutting off the prey's line of escape. Animals such as this wildebeest (right) are sometimes killed with a bite to the neck which crushes the vertebrae. On other occasions, the lion suffocates its prey by gripping on to the throat.

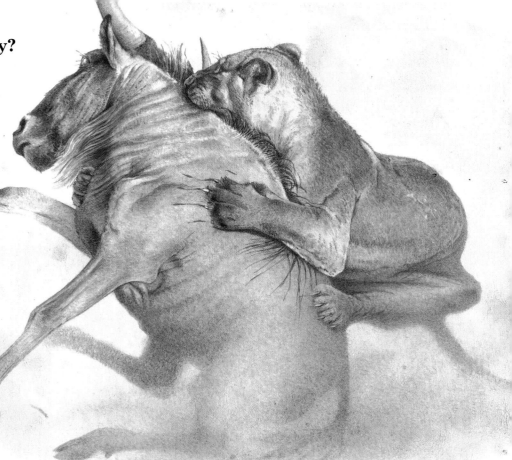

Q How do kangaroos and wallabies run?

A Kangaroos and wallabies run using their large and powerful back legs to hop. The small front legs are used only for feeding and grooming. The long, robust tail helps the animal balance when it is hopping. Some kangaroos can reach speeds of 25 mph or more and are able to hop for long periods of time. Kangaroos live in Australia.

Q How does the porcupine protect itself?

A The sharp, spiny quills of a porcupine are really just specially strengthened hairs. In some species, such as the African porcupine (left), they can reach a length of 20 inches. The quills are so strong that they can cause painful injuries if they are jabbed into a would-be attacker.

NATURE

Q How do musk-oxen protect their young?

A When threatened by enemies, such as wolves, a herd of musk-oxen (right) form a line facing them, or form a circle with the calves in the middle (below). Big males then dash out and jab the attackers with their huge, powerful, curved horns.

Q Why do some animals only come out at night?

A Animals that only come out at night are called nocturnal. They may be nocturnal in order to catch other nocturnal animals or to avoid daytime predators, or both. Nocturnal animals often have large eyes and good eyesight. They also need a keen sense of smell and good hearing to listen for danger.

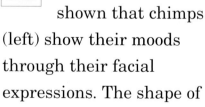

Q How do chimps show their moods?

A Scientists have shown that chimps (left) show their moods through their facial expressions. The shape of the mouth, and whether or not the teeth are bared, are important signals. From top to bottom, the chimps are showing a desire to play, begging for food, intense fear and, lastly, anxiety.

Q How does the honeyguide get its name?

A Honeyguides (below) come from Africa and are so-called because they lead honey badgers and humans to the nests of wild bees using a series of calls. After the nest has been raided for honey, the honeyguide gets the chance to feed on bee grubs from the open nest.

Q Why do animals defend their territory?

A Not all animals have territories but many do. If food is limited, the animal may defend a territory to guard its food supply. With other species, such as these cassowaries (right), the males fight over a territory in which to nest and rear their young. Territorial animals know exactly where the boundaries of their own territory lie.

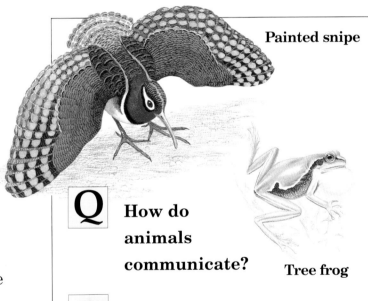

Painted snipe

Tree frog

Q How are young cuckoos reared?

A Female cuckoos (below) lay their eggs in the nests of other birds and then abandon their offspring. The host bird has the task of feeding and rearing the young cuckoo. As it grows up, the young cuckoo tips the host bird's eggs and young from the nest. By the time it is ready to leave the nest, the young cuckoo may be several times the size of its long-suffering foster parent.

Q How do animals communicate?

A Animals signal to each other in two main ways: by using visual signals, such as shape or color, and by sound. Birds, such as the painted snipe, have showy wings which they fan out to make an impression. Many birds sing to advertise their territories or attract a mate. Most frogs can also produce a croaking song to mark their territories or attract a mate.

NATURE

PETS

Q Where do canaries come from?

A In the wild, canaries (above) are found on the Canary Islands off North Africa and the islands of the Azores and Madeira. They have been kept for more than 400 years because they can sing. Breeding in captivity has produced a wide range of different colors. Most captive birds are bright yellow. Their wild relatives are a duller olive-green color and are still found on their native islands.

Q Do pet mice have wild relatives?

A Domesticated pet mice are all descended from the wild house mouse. This animal has lived alongside humans for more than 10,000 years, ever since people began to store grain and other foods. Mice have been kept as pets for several centuries and a range of color varieties (right) has been bred.

Q What is a Manx cat?

A The Manx cat (above) is a very distinctive breed that is best known for its lack of tail. It first came from the Isle of Man, an island in the Irish Sea. Manx cats have long legs for their size with thickset bodies. Their color is like that of a tabby or wild cat, with stripes and blotches of various shades of brown and gray-brown. Manx cats are popular as a show breed but they do not make particularly affectionate pets.

Q How many breeds of dogs are there?

A There are over 300 different breeds of dogs, and each country has its own system of grouping them. In the United Kingdom and Australia the main groups are: hounds, terriers, toys, gun, working and utility. In America dogs are also grouped into sporting and nonsporting. European countries use different groupings.

American foxhound (hound)

Bouvier des Flandres (working)

Q Are there different breeds of rabbit?

A There are many different breeds and varieties of rabbit, all
descended from the wild rabbit. About 2,000 years ago,
the Romans brought rabbits from their native Spain, Portugal
and southern France to raise them for their
meat. Rabbits now live in many parts of
the world. People also breed rabbits
for their fur and for show.

Q What is a Persian cat?

A A Persian (right) is the
best-known breed of
long-haired cat. It was first
bred in Europe in the 1800s
by crossing cats imported from
Persia (now Iran) and from
Angora in Turkey. The breed has a
long, silky coat and a broad head. A
Persian cat's legs are short but the body
is broad and robust. Although this
example is black-and-white, Persians
come in several different colors.

Irish setter
(gundog)

Great dane
(utility)

Lakeland terrier
(terrier)

Chihuahua
(toy)

NATURE

PLANT LIFE

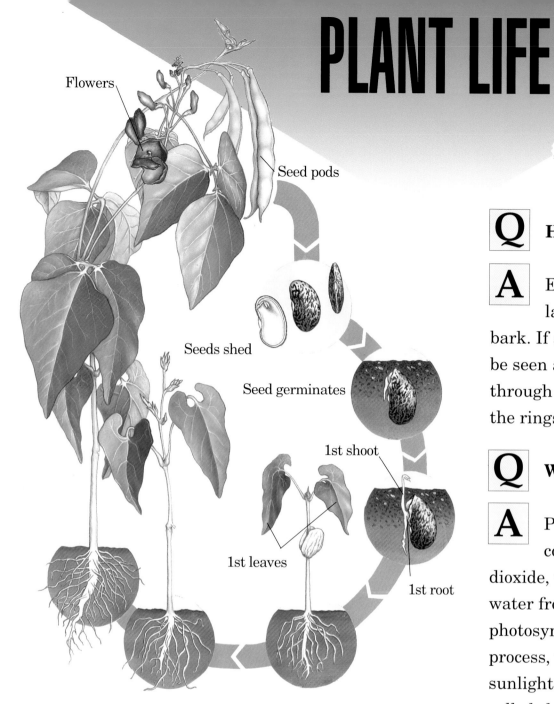

Flowers

Seed pods

Seeds shed

Seed germinates

1st shoot

1st leaves

1st root

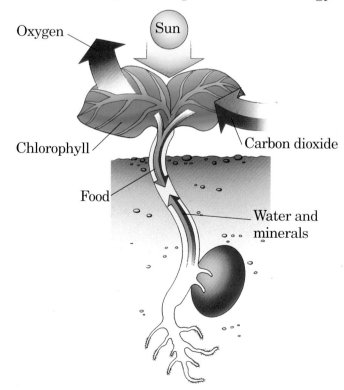

Q How can you tell a tree's age?

A Every year a tree grows a new layer of wood just beneath the bark. If a tree is cut down, the layers can be seen as rings in the cross-section through the stump (above). By counting the rings you can tell its age.

Q Why do plants need sunlight?

A Plants make their own food by combining a gas called carbon dioxide, which they get from the air, with water from the soil. This process is called photosynthesis (below). To power the process, the plant uses the energy of sunlight. A green pigment in the leaves called chlorophyll traps the Sun's energy.

Oxygen

Sun

Chlorophyll

Carbon dioxide

Food

Water and minerals

Q How does a plant complete its life cycle?

A Every year, plants (above) produce large numbers of seeds which fall to the ground. Many die but some will germinate. Tiny roots and shoots grow from the seed and soon the plant increases in size. As the plant grows larger, more and more leaves are produced and eventually flowers appear. Pollen from male flowers fertilizes female flowers and the base of the flower begins to swell. It is here that this year's seeds are being made, completing the plant's life cycle.

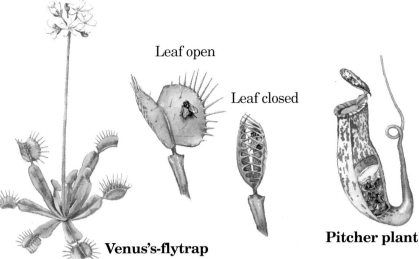

Q Which plants eat animals?

A Venus's-flytraps and pitcher plants (right) can absorb nutrients from animals. Venus's-flytraps have leaves which trap insects and digest them. Pitcher plants have flask-shaped leaves in which water collects. Insects fall in and drown.

Leaf open

Leaf closed

Venus's-flytrap

Pitcher plant

Q What are fruit "pips"?

A Fruit pips are the seeds of the plant which produced the fruit. There are many types of fruit but most are juicy and nutritious, which make animals eat them. The seed may be swallowed whole and passed out in the animal's droppings later on. In this way, the plant has its seeds scattered, or dispersed.

Q Why do plants produce flowers?

A Plants produce flowers (below) to reproduce and create a new generation. Flowers bear the male and female parts. Many flowers have colors and scents that attract insects. The insects take male pollen to the female parts of other flowers. The pollen of some flowers is carried by the wind.

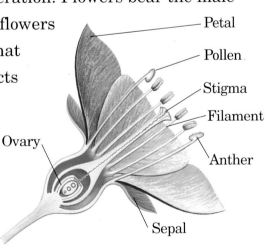

Petal

Pollen

Stigma

Filament

Ovary

Anther

Sepal

Q How do daffodils survive the winter?

A Daffodils have leaves and flowers above ground only for a few months each spring. During the winter they live as onion-shaped bulbs buried in the ground. Bulbs are protected from winter frosts by the soil above them.

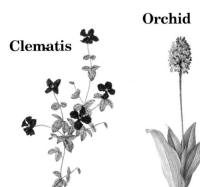

Bulb cross-section

Fritillaria

Clematis

Orchid

Silver birch

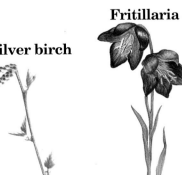
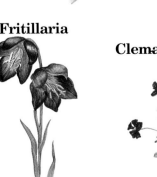

NATURE

FORCES & ENERGY

Slow-moving neutron

Uranium-235

Uranium-236

Fission fragment — Fission fragment

Uranium-235

Q **What is gravity?**

A Gravity is the force that pulls everything to Earth. Galileo showed that gravity makes all objects fall equally fast. When he dropped a light ball and a heavy ball from the leaning Tower of Pisa (above), they hit the ground at the same instant.

Q **What is an Archimedes' Screw used for?**

A The Archimedes' Screw (below) was invented by Archimedes in Ancient Greece. It is used for lifting water. One end of the screw is dipped into water. By turning the handle, the water is raised up inside the tube until it spills out of the top.

Q **How is energy released inside a nuclear reactor?**

A A slow-moving neutron is made to hit an atom of uranium-235 (above). It combines with the nucleus at the center of the atom, forming uranium-236. This splits into two particles called fission fragments, releasing a burst of energy and three more neutrons, which split more uranium atoms.

Q **What forces act on an airplane in flight?**

A Four forces act on an airplane. Its weight acts downwards. The thrust of its engines pushes it forwards. Lift created by its wings acts upwards. Drag tries to slow it down. Thrust must overcome drag, and lift must overcome weight, if a plane is to fly.

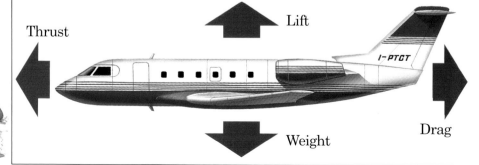

Thrust

Lift

Weight

Drag

Q How does a space rocket work?

A A rocket motor propels a rocket by burning fuel mixed with an oxidizer. The oxidizer contains oxygen, which is necessary for burning. The Ariane V rocket (below), burns hydrogen fuel with oxygen. The hot gas produced rushes out of the motor nozzles, forcing the rocket upwards.

Q What is a force?

A A force is something that changes an object's speed or direction. Forces always exist in pairs acting in opposite directions. When a rifle is fired (below right), the rifle kicks back as the bullet flies forwards. A heavier football player running faster applies a greater force than a lighter, slower player (below left).

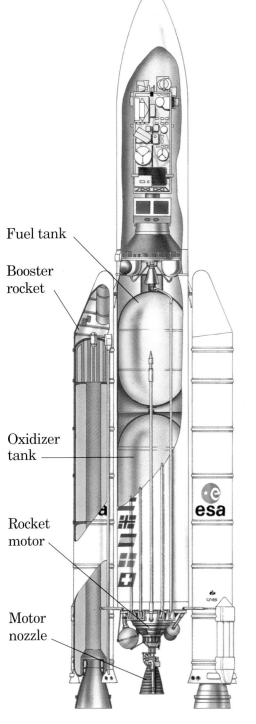

Fuel tank

Booster rocket

Oxidizer tank

Rocket motor

Motor nozzle

Q What is friction?

A Friction is a force that stops surfaces sliding across each other easily. Sometimes friction is helpful. It allows our shoes to grip the ground. Without friction walking would be impossible. But friction can also be a problem because it wears out the moving parts of machines.

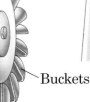

Q How does a turbine work?

A A turbine (right) is a machine that uses gas or liquid to make a shaft turn. Water hitting the buckets of a Pelton wheel drives the buckets around and turns the shaft. Wind spins the blades of a wind turbine. Wind and water turbines often drive electricity generators.

Wind turbine

Rotor blade

Generator

Pelton wheel

Water jet

Shaft

Buckets

SCIENCE & TECHNOLOGY

ELECTRICITY & MAGNETISM

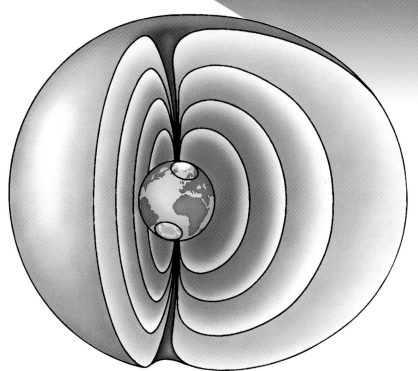

Q How do electric vehicles work?

A An electric car (above) works by using electricity stored in batteries to power an electric motor connected to the car's wheels. Electric trains are supplied with electricity from wires above the track or a third rail beside the track. It powers electric motors that turn the wheels.

Q What is a magnetic field?

A A magnetic field is a region of forces that exists around a magnet. The field can be drawn as a series of curved lines, called lines of force, joining the magnet's north and south poles. The Earth behaves like a magnet. Its magnetic field (above), caused by electric currents inside the liquid part of its core, stretches thousands of miles into space.

Q How are magnets made?

A An iron bar contains molecular magnets pointing in all directions. If the bar is placed inside a coil carrying an electric current, the molecular magnets line up with the coil's magnetic field. The bar has now become a magnet (right).

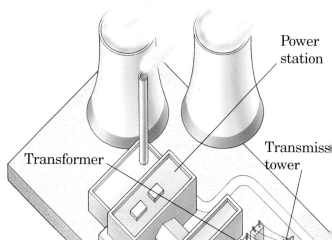

Power station

Transformer

Transmiss tower

Q How do we get electricity?

A Electricity made at power stations (above) is distributed along cables at a very high voltage. The cables cross the countryside, strung between tall transmission towers. Electricity is distributed inside towns by underground cables. Before it can be used, its voltage must be reduced. The final voltage varies from country to country.

A An electric motor is made of a coil of wire inside a magnet. The coil is free to turn. When an electric current flows through the coil, it magnetizes the coil. This magnetic field pushes against the magnetic field produced by the surrounding magnet and this makes the coil spin.

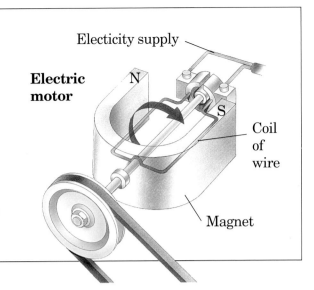

Electicity supply

Electric motor

N

S

Coil of wire

Magnet

Q **How does a doorbell work?**

A When the bell push button (below) is pressed, the coil becomes magnetized. The iron rod shoots out of the coil and strikes the short chime. When the push button is released, the rod swings back into the coil and hits the long chime.

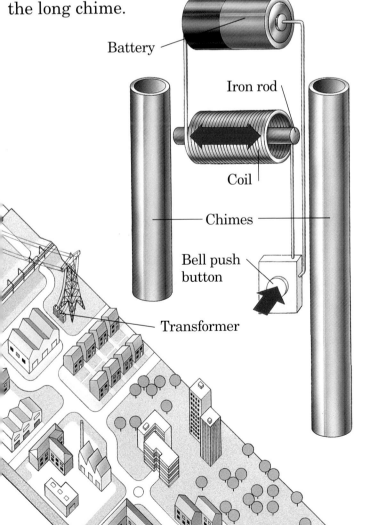

Battery

Iron rod

Coil

Chimes

Bell push button

Transformer

Q **What is inside a battery?**

A Cars and trucks use a type of battery called a storage battery (below). It contains flat plates of lead and lead oxide dipped in sulfuric acid. When the battery is connected to a circuit, a chemical reaction between the plates and the acid makes an electric current flow around the circuit. A storage battery is recharged by passing an electric current through it.

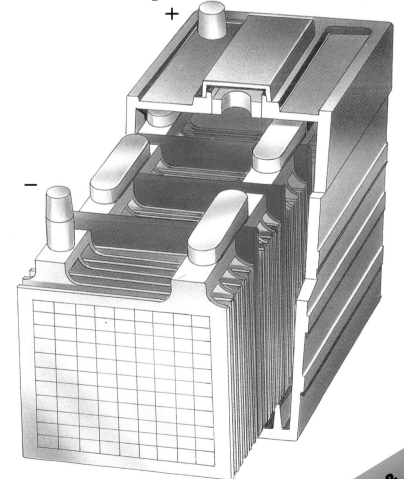

+

−

43

SCIENCE & TECHNOLOGY

HEAT & LIGHT

Q What is light?

A Light is a form of energy. It is composed of waves of electric and magnetic vibrations that our eyes can detect. The different colors (below) are produced by light waves of different lengths. We are unable to see waves shorter than blue light and longer than red.

Gas burner

Gas bottle

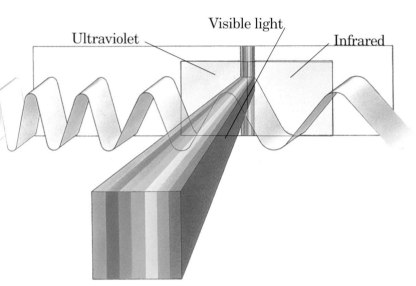

Ultraviolet

Visible light

Infrared

Q How does a hot air balloon rise?

A A gas burner supplied by gas from bottles in the balloon's basket (above) heats the air inside the balloon. As the air warms up, it expands. The thinner air inside the balloon is lighter than the surrounding air, so the balloon floats upwards.

Q How fast does light travel?

A The speed of light is 186,000 mps, faster than anything else in the universe. Light takes roughly 8½ minutes to travel from the Sun (below) to the Earth. Looking at distant objects allows us to look back in time. When we look at a remote galaxy, we see it as it was when the light left it.

Q How does a laser work?

A Light is normally composed of different wavelengths (colors) mixed at random. A laser produces an intense beam of high-energy light in which all the light is of the same wavelength. The process is started by an electric current or a flash of light from a flash tube which causes a gas or ruby rod (below) to send out the laser beam.

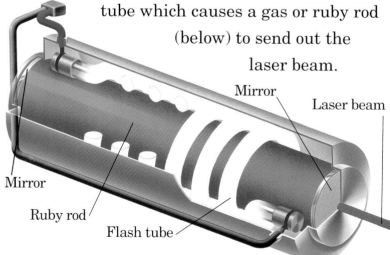

Mirror

Laser beam

Mirror

Ruby rod

Flash tube

Q What are thermals?

A Birds can often be seen gliding in tight circles, being carried upwards by rising columns of air called thermals (right). Ground heated by the Sun warms the air above it. The warm air rises, sucking cool air in below it. That, too, is warmed and rises up. Glider pilots use thermals. They circle and climb inside one thermal, then glide to the next (below).

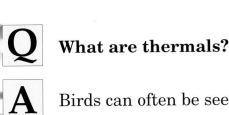

Bird's flight path

Thermal

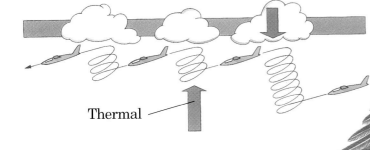

Thermal

Q How does a fluorescent tube work?

A A hot wire inside the tube sends out particles called electrons, which crash into atoms of mercury gas. The mercury atoms give out invisible ultraviolet radiation. The white phosphorus coating in the tube (below) changes this into bright visible light.

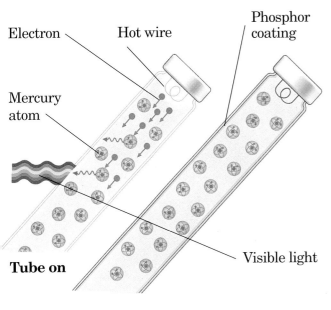

Electron

Hot wire

Phosphor coating

Mercury atom

Visible light

Tube on

Tube off

Q How does heat move along a metal bar?

A When something is heated, its atoms vibrate. If one end of a metal bar is heated, the atoms at that end vibrate more than the atoms at the cold end. The vibration spreads along the bar from atom to atom. The spread of heat in this way is called conduction. Metals are good conductors of heat.

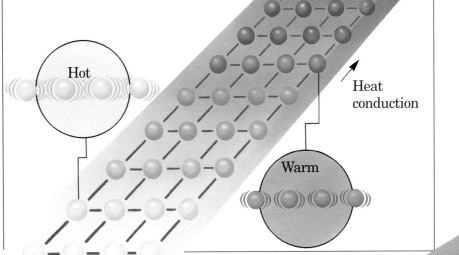

Cold

Hot

Warm

Heat conduction

SCIENCE & TECHNOLOGY

SHIPS

A The world's largest ships are cargo vessels. The largest of these are the supertankers that carry oil around the world (left). The largest ship afloat today is the oil tanker *Jahre Viking*. It is 1,502 feet long and 26 feet across. Its cavernous hull extends 82 feet below the water-line. When it is fully loaded with crude oil, it weighs 621,500 tons.

Q How does a lifeboat work?

A When a distress message is received, a lifeboat is quickly on its way. It may be launched from a carriage, down a slipway, or from a permanent mooring which the crew reaches by small boat. Lifeboats are designed to operate in rough seas. Most can turn themselves the right way up if they capsize.

Q What is inside a submarine?

A A submarine (below) contains a pressurized compartment where the crew lives and works. The space between this and the outer hull contains a series of fuel, oil, water, waste and ballast tanks. When the ballast tanks are flooded with sea water, the submarine becomes heavier than the surrounding water and sinks. When air is pumped into the tanks, forcing the water out, the submarine becomes lighter and rises.

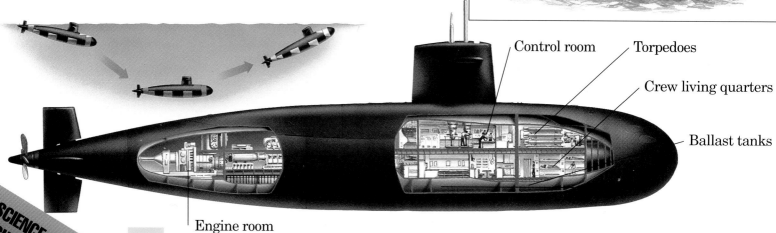

Control room · Torpedoes · Crew living quarters · Ballast tanks · Engine room

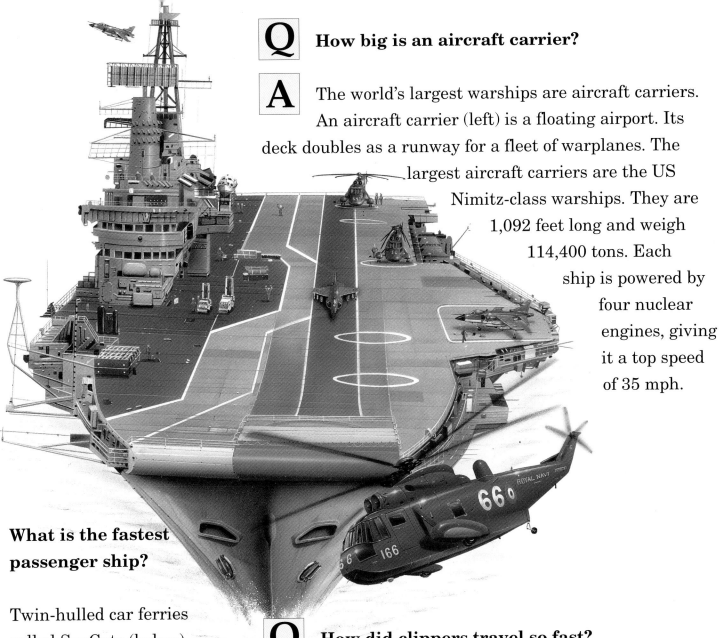

Q How big is an aircraft carrier?

A The world's largest warships are aircraft carriers. An aircraft carrier (left) is a floating airport. Its deck doubles as a runway for a fleet of warplanes. The largest aircraft carriers are the US Nimitz-class warships. They are 1,092 feet long and weigh 114,400 tons. Each ship is powered by four nuclear engines, giving it a top speed of 35 mph.

Q What is the fastest passenger ship?

A Twin-hulled car ferries called SeaCats (below) cruise at a speed of 40 mph. They can reach a top speed of 48 mph. SeaCats are powered by water-jet engines. Instead of propellers, they pump water backwards at great speed to propel the ship forwards.

Q How did clippers travel so fast?

A Clippers (below) were the fastest sailing ships of the 19th century. Their narrow hulls slipped through the water easily. They carried a large sail area to catch as much wind as possible. The fastest clippers, such as the *Cutty Sark*, carried almost 3,600 square yards of sail and could reach a speed of nearly 20 mph.

FLIGHT

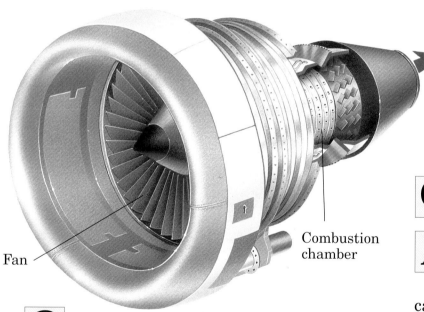

Q How does an airplane stay in the air?

A Airplanes (left) can fly because of the shape of their wings. The top of the wing is more curved than the bottom. Air rushing over the top of the wings travels farther and faster than the air flowing underneath. This produces lower air pressure above the wings than below them (below), causing the wings to lift.

Jet of hot air

Airflow

Q What happens before take-off?

A An airliner (below) is carefully prepared for each flight. The passenger cabin is cleaned. Meals and luggage are loaded. The fuel tanks are filled. Engineers check the plane and the crew make their preflight checks.

Combustion chamber

Fan

Q How does a jet engine work?

A A large spinning fan at the front of the engine (above) sucks in air. The air is then compressed and heated by burning fuel in the combustion chamber. This makes the air expand quickly. A jet of hot air rushes out of the back of the engine and pushes the airplane forwards.

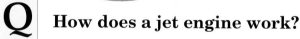

Q What did the first airplane look like?

A The first airplane, called *Flyer 1* (right), flew in 1903. It was made from wood. It had two wings covered with fabric, one above the other, and the pilot lay down on the lower wing to fly it.

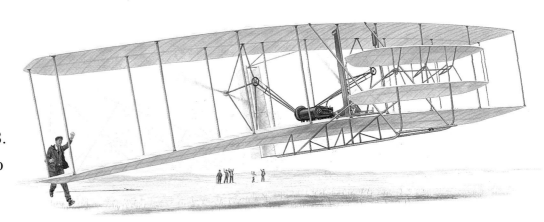

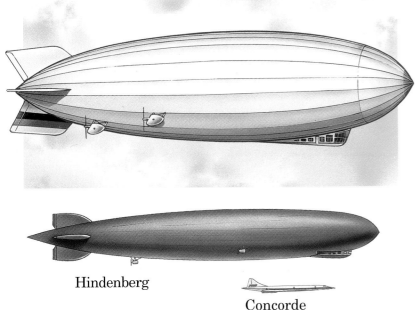

Hindenberg

Concorde

Q What is a Zeppelin?

A A Zeppelin (left) is a giant airship named after its inventor, Count Ferdinand von Zeppelin. The Zeppelins were built in Germany between 1900 and the 1930s. The biggest passenger-carrying Zeppelins were the *Graf Zeppelin* and the *Hindenberg*. They carried passengers across the Atlantic Ocean. Zeppelins could fly without wings because they were filled with hydrogen gas. This is lighter than air and made the airships float upward.

Q Which aircraft can carry the largest cargo?

A The Airbus Super Transporter A300-600ST Beluga has the largest cargo hold of any aircraft. It can carry up to 45 tons of cargo in a hold that is 120 feet long and up to 24 feet wide. Belugas are built from Airbus A300 airliners. They replace the Super Guppy transporter (below). The Super Guppies were built to transport parts of the giant Saturn 5 moon rockets.

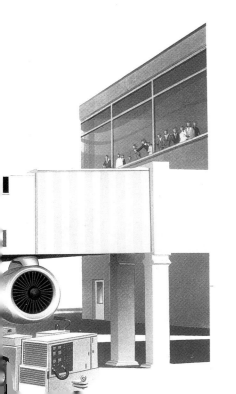

AIRBUS SKYLINK

SCIENCE & TECHNOLOGY

LAND TRAVEL

Q How are heavy loads carried by road?

A The largest and heaviest loads are carried on a special low trailer pulled by a powerful tractor unit (right). This vehicle has six axles to spread the load. The tractor unit has six sets of wheels. Four of them are driven by the engine to give maximum power.

Tractor unit

Trailer

Q How does a refrigeration truck keep its cargo cold?

A Cargoes that have to be kept cold are transported in a refrigerated truck (below). The insulated trailer has a refrigeration unit on the front. Liquid coolant flows through pipes in the trailer and absorbs heat from the cargo. The coolant returns to the refrigeration unit and gives up its heat to the outside air. It is then compressed to turn it back into a cold liquid and recirculated through the trailer.

Refrigeration unit

Q Which were the largest ever steam trains?

A The largest steam locomotives ever built were five giants called Big Boys. They were built in the 1940s for the Union Pacific Railroad. The locomotive and its coal tender (right) were almost 130 feet long, 10 feet wide and 16 feet high. They weighed nearly 600 tons. They pulled up to 4,400 tons of freight in the Rock Mountains.

SCIENCE & TECHNOLOGY

Q Can the Sun power vehicles?

A Sunshine can be turned into electricity by solar cells. A vehicle covered with solar cells can produce enough electricity to drive an electric motor. A solar-powered bicycle crossed Australia at an average speed of 31 mph. The fastest solar-powered car, Sunraycer, was capable of a top speed of 48 mph.

Q What is the fastest train?

A The world's fastest train in service today is the French TGV (Train à Grande Vitesse) Atlantique. The first of these high-speed electric trains was introduced in 1981. On May 18, 1990, a TGV Atlantique train (right) reached the record-breaking speed of 319 mph between Courtalain and Tours. In everyday passenger service, TGV Atlantiques normally travel at up to 186 mph.

Q What is a supercar?

A Supercars are the super sports models of the car world. They are fast, powerful and very expensive. The Ferrari F40 (right) is certainly a supercar. One of the world's fastest production cars, it can reach a top speed of 202 mph. One special feature is that the engine is behind the driver.

SCIENCE & TECHNOLOGY

BUILDINGS

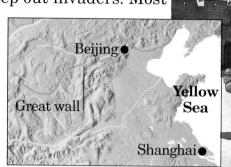

Q Why was the Great Wall of China built?

A The Great Wall of China (right) was built by Chinese emperors to keep out invaders. Most of it was built by the emperor Qin Shih Huang Ti between 221 B.C. and 204 B.C. The wall finally reached a length of over 3,700 miles. Much of the wall is still standing today.

Beijing●

Great wall

Yellow Sea

Shanghai●

Q What is Abu Simbel?

A Abu Simbel is a place in Egypt where the Egyptian king, Rameses II, built two temples in about 1,250 B.C. They were cut into blocks and rebuilt on higher ground in the 1960s when the rising waters of Lake Nasser threatened to cover them.

Q Which building materials did the Romans use?

A Most Roman buildings (right) were made from bricks and concrete. Stone and glass were more expensive, so they were only used for important buildings. Romans were experts at building arches. They built a temporary wooden arch first, then covered it with bricks and poured concrete over the top. Finally the wooden arch was removed.

Concrete

Bricks

Wooden arch

Glass window

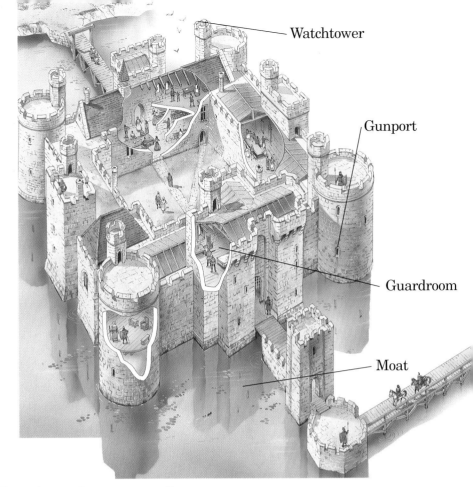

Watchtower

Gunport

Guardroom

Moat

Q Why were castles built?

A Castles were built to protect the people who lived in them. They were often built on hilltops or surrounded by water to make them easier to defend. Bodiam Castle (right) was a manor house in Sussex, England, that was strengthened to resist French attacks in the 1300s.

Q Why was the Statue of Liberty built?

A The Statue of Liberty (above) stands on an island at the entrance to New York harbor. It was a gift from France to the United States in 1886 to celebrate the American Revolution. It is made from copper sheeting, and with its base stands 305 feet high. Its rusting iron skeleton was replaced by stainless steel in the 1980s.

Q What is a skyscraper?

A A skyscraper is a very tall building supported by a steel frame inside it. The world's most famous skyscraper is the Empire State Building in New York (right). Built in 1931, it stands 1,250 feet tall. The tallest skyscrapers today are the twin Petronas Towers in Malaysia. They stand 1,483 feet high, 499 feet taller than the Eiffel Tower in Paris, France, which was itself the tallest building in the world until 1930.

Eiffel Tower | Empire State Building | Petronas Towers

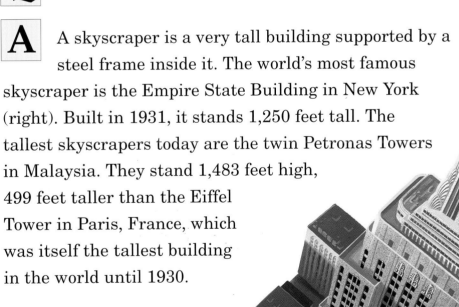

SCIENCE & TECHNOLOGY

Entrance

Burial chamber

Q How long did it take to build the Great Pyramid?

A The Great Pyramid was built as a tomb for King Khufu, also called Cheops. It is at Giza, in Egypt. Work began in about 2,575 B.C. It took thousands of people about 25 years to assemble it (right) from 2.3 million blocks of stone. It weighs over 6.6 million tons and is today 453 feet high. The Great Pyramid was the tallest building in the world for 4,000 years.

Q What type of bridge is the Sydney Harbour Bridge?

A The Sydney Harbour Bridge in Australia is a steel arch bridge spanning 1,650 feet. It is not the longest steel arch, but it is the widest. It carries two railway tracks, eight traffic lanes, a cycle track and a footpath. It was opened in 1932.

Q What is the Eiffel Tower?

A The Eiffel Tower (right) is one of the most famous French landmarks. Designed by the engineer Alexandre-Gustave Eiffel, it was built in 1889 to celebrate the 100th anniversary of the French Revolution. It stands 984 feet high, and is a slender pyramid made from 7,700 tons of iron girders.

SCIENCE & TECHNOLOGY

Q How is the space shuttle moved to its launch pad?

A The space shuttle (left) is prepared for launch inside a building at the Kennedy Space Center in Florida. It is moved to the launch pad 4 miles away by the world's largest crawler transporter. This giant is 131 feet long and weighs nearly 3,000 tons. It travels on four double caterpillar tracks. The tracks are moved by electric motors driven by generators powered by diesel engines.

Q What is an oil platform?

A Oil platforms are offshore drilling rigs which stand on the seabed. The tallest is the Auger platform in the Gulf of Mexico. It stands in 2,860 feet of water. The Gullfaks C platform (above) in the North Sea stands on concrete pillars and supports production equipment, loading derricks, and a helicopter pad.

Q How does a flood barrier work?

A The Thames Barrier (right) was opened in 1984 to protect London from flooding. It consists of eight gates each weighing 4,070 tons. They normally lie on the river bed. If there is any danger of flooding, the gates are rotated to raise them up against the flood water.

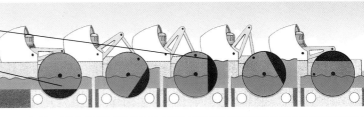

Gate raised

Gate lowered

SCIENCE & TECHNOLOGY

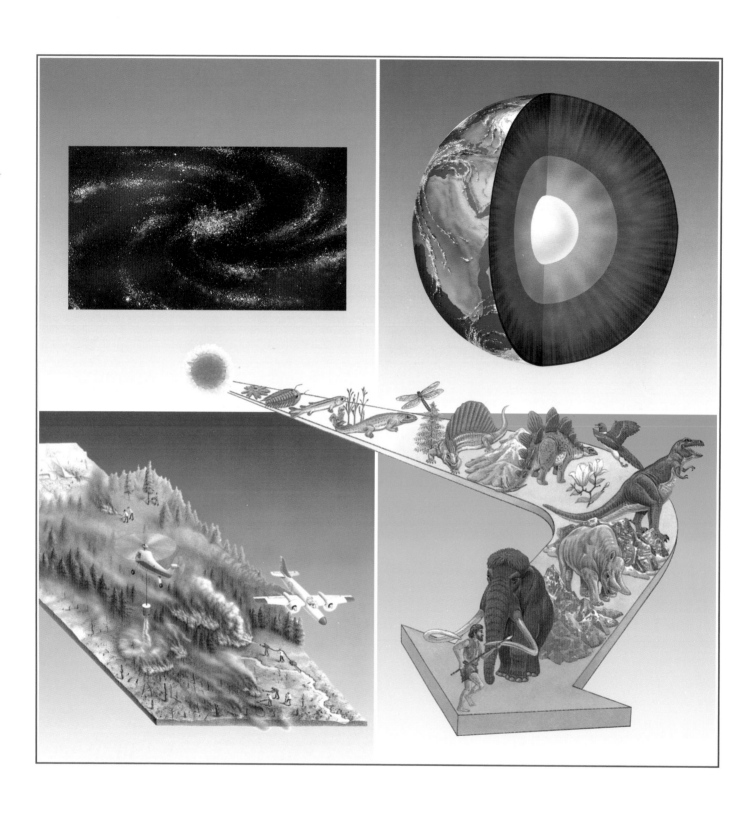